DUCKS
& GEESE

D1254984

DUCKS & GEESE

By S.G.B. Tennant, Jr.
Photography by Arie deZanger

WILLOW CREEK PRESS

Minocqua, Wisconsin

Published by Willow Creek Press
P.O. Box 147
Minocqua, Wisconsin 54548

Designed by Heather M. McElwain

For information on other Willow Creek titles, call 1-800-850-9453

Library of Congress Cataloging-in-Publication Data
Tennant, S.G.B.
    Ducks & geese / by S.G.B. Tennant ; photography by Arie deZanger.
    p.   cm.
    Includes index.
    ISBN 1-57223-202-1
    1. Cookery (Duck)   2. Cookery (Game)   I. Title.   II. Title: Ducks and geese.   III. Series.
TX750.5.D82T46 1999
641.6'91--dc21   99-18071
                                                                      CIP

Printed in Canada

TABLE OF CONTENTS

ACKNOWLEDGMENTS

We all owe commendation to the thousands of tireless volunteers at Ducks Unlimited. Their direct contributions to the wild duck population, the wetlands of North America, and the spirit of conservationism have benefited thousands of species of birds and wildlife. The future of game cookery is bright because of their foresight. Join up if you care!

Ducks Unlimited National Headquarters
Ducks Unlimited, Inc.
One Waterfowl Way
Memphis, Tennessee 38120
(800) 4-5-D-U-C-K-S or (901)758-3825

We wish to thank a few enthusiastic suppliers who helped in the production of this book:

D'Artagnan [(800) 327-8246] was the purveyor of ducks used in the photographs throughout these pages.

Waterford–Wedgwood [(800) 677-7860] provided the china used in the Black Grape Sauce, Pressed Duck and Peking Roll illustrations.

P.J. Flowers and Designers Guild [(212) 840-3100] arranged the table linens under the snow goose and specklebelly goose illustrations.

INTRODUCTION

Mr. Tom O'Connor loved to eat teal. Green wing, blue wing teal, even a cinnamon teal occasionally, but for all of his long life he had lived on his family's ranch, shooting birds in the fall and working cattle in the spring. What he loved most was teal roasted in a ceramic clay pot. His favorite recipe wasn't complicated, but it brought three important tastes to life in a dish that was simple and satisfying.

Toward the end of his days afield Mr. Tom delegated the catching and the cooking to others, but he wanted to be sure there was fresh duck, root vegetables, and a little "splash of wine that wouldn't offend a preacher."

And in a sympathetic sort of way that's the basis for the presentations of ducks and geese that are assembled here. This book is a collection of techniques and recipes borrowed from thoughtful chefs who have prepared these wonderful birds over the generations. In each case there is a history that is as important as the details.

My involvement in game cooking came from having a lot of birds and a little bit of ambition. I began to hear about great recipes, and I began to visit a few great restaurants. And then I got the chance to travel the world of game cooking, and I started taking notes.

One thing I found is that there are no new recipes. And few new ingredients! I leave it to the anthropologists to say whether the limits of taste are defined by nature or nurture, but good recipes have something in common. They all grew up in a certain time, and a certain place, and so long as they are faithful to their own cuisine, they will endure.

Everybody gets amended along life's course, and recipes aren't any different. Many of these can be traced directly to 19th-century Britain, or France or Germany or China, but they have all had to do time in my kitchen. I am even prepared to offer a salute to the new "California Cuisine," on a case-by-case basis.

Any collection of duck and goose recipes risks offending everyone. Hunters have their own favorite methods of preparation, and a fierce loyalty to their birds and their way of life. Chefs and restaurant-goers have grown accustomed to reliably plump, tender meat from the domestic bird whose flavor is rich and never varies.

So we have made allowances here, and adjustments, but all of these recipes are intended for simple kitchens staffed by one or perhaps two energetic, vaguely bourgeois adults, who are sufficiently self-reliant that they can spend their discretionary time in the pursuit of pleasurable dining.

I have been very fortunate in this undertaking to have the very upscale photographer Arie deZanger and his charming spouse, Wilma, looking over my culinary shoulder as usual during this book, and it has been great fun working with them.

It is particularly exciting to me that ducks and geese are now back on the radar screen of food fashion, and with dependable domestic supplies, and the wild population showing signs of sustainable growth in recent years, ducks and geese are on the comeback.

These birds are meant to be eaten at the happiest of times, as I so often remember. And I hope that both the locals in the swamp and the "foodies" in the suburbs will all enjoy this "Call from the Sky."

I am honored to be able to dedicate these pages to Borden and Gene and Arthur and Maureen, who kept the kitchen fires burning.

Good cooking!

— *S.G.B. Tennant, Jr.*
Helena, Texas

"THE VOYAGE OF THE PAYSON

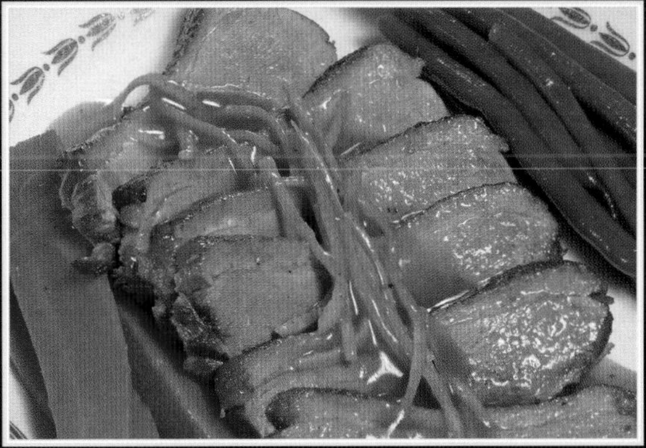

The broad shallows of Espiritu Santo Bay are blessed in winter with what seems like every red-headed duck in the Central Flyway. They arrive in Deep South Texas in November to ply their diving ways up and down the marshes like a great bee-winged plague of locusts. From miles away across the bay you can pick out the flights of redheads. At one moment they mass together and fly straight up in crowds so thick they blacken the sky. In the next instant they single out and fly in long, low level lines, only a few feet over the water, nipping the points of the scalloped grass islands.

I was twelve years old when I saw it, driving down with my Dad on our first duck hunt together. There has been nothing like it since. We clambered aboard the old tug named "The Payson," dragging duffels and ice chests onto what was to be our home for the next three days, and would become a temple of all that was good and holy on this earth for me for the next fifty years.

And this was the beginning of that voyage and of many encounters with the splendid ways that duck has come to the table ever since. The wild ducks, and those high 'ole memories of an island duck camp, where oysters 'cooned up from the shallow reefs hissed and popped open on a bed of coals sautéed in their own juice are indelible images.

But make no mistake, duck hunting is for the camaraderie, the primal sublimation with nature, the bonding of hunters, or whatever else inspires you, but it is not about cuisine. The fact that wild ducks around a campfire taste wonderful is largely due to the ambiance. The birds themselves are invariably older, tougher, and less meaty than the domestic bird.

The ultimate presentation of duck as haute cuisine developed over generations, and for best effect requires young, plump, carefully selected birds. Virtually all thoughtful duck recipes were developed on domestic birds, although hunters have adapted most of them, and still loyally claim that the wild birds they have taken are superior, gristle notwithstanding.

This wasn't always the case, of course. The canvasback duck before World War I was so honored for its flavor that it was served at presidential banquets, and lauded by Escoffier for the rich subtlety of its flavor. But the ravages of time and disease wiped out the wild celery that made up the canvasback's principle diet, with a similar fate occurring to other waterfowl, like the Brant, to the extent that these birds of today are merely ordinary, if not downright inedible.

And we're lucky to have any birds at all to hunt! Ducks Unlimited and other highly motivated groups can take all the credit for raising the alarm, and then raising the money. They reversed a tide of gloom that washed over many species of animals and breeds of wild ducks and threatened the very culture of hunting. The ducks owe a lot to fellows like John Kelsey, frantic, brilliant auction chairman, scrounging up fortunes for the cause.

As a nation we seemed to expect this bounty from the sky, a munificence of sport and food. In the heyday of market gunning at the turn of the century, thousands of wild ducks were shot and sold, and eaten indiscriminately, but this should not be taken as evidence of their culinary value. Bufflehead, whistlers, broad bills, old squaws and even mergansers by the barrel-load were shipped to market every day without scruple or distinction. Many were shot but few were savored.

Elmer Crowell carved magnificent duck decoys in the 1920s, including sets of dozens of mergansers, but surely he couldn't have eaten more than one! And that's the point here. The pressed duck, the *jus à l'orange*, the pâtés and Szechuan ducks of culinary fame — virtually the entire canon of duck cookery as we know it — was created for domestic birds.

Most duck recipes are convertible, but older wild birds develop more gristle in the meat fibers, and tougher muscles as the years go on. Such specimens are best braised and sauced heavily, or used in gumbos.

This doesn't keep duck hunters from trying, however, and as my old pal, the late Judge Tom Gee, once observed, "...there are more duck presses in hunting clubs around America than in all the restaurants put together." It is somehow in the nature of duck hunters that they want to imagine that in their isolated, self-sufficient redoubt, no matter the weather, they are surrounded with the best things in life.

Judge Gee and I once sat in the freezing rain waiting for ducks in the company of my old shooting pal Irvin Barnhart. We were wet and cold and the weather was worse. The Judge talked about the "jus à l'orange" sauce scheduled for the evening meal.

"Will we have that splendid, warm sauce," the Judge said, waving his hand vaguely toward the camp, "back in that dry, little camphouse around that jolly gas heater in the kitchen?"

Now Irvin Barnhart has heard every hunting story in the book spoken in Swahili, Inuit, Afrikaans and "bush-speak," and he certainly knows a dodge when he hears one. He had also seen the jar of extra-peel marmalade I left out on the kitchen table back at camp. "Not much chance tonight, Judge," Irvin said. "It's a warm-weather sauce. Needs those oranges kissed by the glowing Mediterranean sun. Can't you feel the rays?"

The true Seville orange originally prescribed for the sauce is often hard to come by, so a judicious blend of lemon juice will balance the dull sweetness of our native oranges. Grapefruit juice combinations also bring the taste right, and lime works, because nothing is sacred or beyond compromise in the pursuit of taste.

Some chefs call the sauce "Bigarade" (if the bird was roasted or fried), as distinguished from duck "à l'orange"(if the bird was braised) — but by whichever name, the sauce is built on the cooking juices, and topped with a tingle of orange rind, and often a splash of orange liqueur.

We got all this from the French, who have always made their sauces out of whatever they had on hand in abundance, such as grapes, and then named them fancifully after the fact.

In the late sixties, before the French Riviera was overrun by development, there was a casual tone to the off-road villages, and at the time of the harvest you could count on the vineyard keeper's wife, the *vigneronne*, cobbling together a rich black grape sauce to accompany a barnyard duckling of the year.

And in the joy of the last harvest of the year they found the last mangoes sent up from India and Larkspur from the vendor's stall. The breasts of muscovy were served, and the legs and thighs put by as confit to be returned as hearty bit players in the soups and cassoulets served out during the winter.

That's a very French-bourgeois attitude toward home cooking, and one that carried across the seas and into the bayou culture of southern Louisiana, because around the Bayou Teche, duck and coot and crab are "found" food. The scents and sounds of the Cajun kitchen are based on a pioneer's endemic frugality, and an unashamed joy in the spicy cooking that is their heritage.

Mane Cernac presided over a sort of Cajun–French kitchen at the back end of his family's duck-shooting barge. Not much went to waste in that kitchen, and every bird that flew by was a candidate for the pot.

And the coot they used in the gumbo isn't a goose or a duck, but rather a small, black member of the Rail clan. The Cajuns recognize how tasty they were and call them *pull-doo*, a corruption of the French *poulet d'eau*, or water chicken.

A gumbo is not a stew, as every Cajun cook will tell you. It needs a roux, and it needs okra. After that the addition of filé is sometimes disputed, but always tasty. Gumbos don't improve with more than an hour of cooking, and the flavors blend because the correct balance is established before anything goes into the pot.

My late colleague A.J. McClane was another duck hunter with high culinary ambitions. He was as intense about his cooking as he was about his fishing, and several of the illustrations in his last cookbook were taken here at the ranch. McClane cheerfully admitted to three distinct variations on his own pressed duck recipe. His favorite being, of course, "the one we're cooking now!"

Everyone likes to imagine themselves at Paris' oldest restaurant, the Tour d'Argent, with the flying table rolling up beside you. The legs of the press bear a casting of the restaurant name on the left, and a mysterious "Frederic" on the right, which if you inquire in perfect French you may learn is "Frederic Delair, deceased, the Maitre d' Hotel" who made the dish popular, serving George Sand, de Musset and other French luminaries in the last century.

The point of the press is to get all the essential juices of the cooked bird into a sauce that can be cooked down to contrast with the meat. Per force they used only yearling, domestic, whole birds, cooked rare, recently breasted, and — please allow me to add in the classical form of the recipe — recently strangled. Not many wild duck hunters can meet that list of ingredients!

It has become our habit to serve the sliced breasts over a very dense, whole wheat *pan de mie* type bread I call Duck Press Bread. The fashion of using bread originated in some of the older American duck clubs, but this bread has a more durable and savory crumb.

The domestic duck also lends itself easily to ballotines. Using the boning technique illustrated in the culinary procedures section here, and with the additions of parboiled red cabbage and sausage, the chef can bring the crispy bird back to the table, or to a cold buffet. (And that's important when your competitive horse-riding career is as far behind you as is mine.) It is still possible to find great pleasure on a Sunday afternoon in trotting out a duck terrine to dress up the tailgate picnic following my daughters' pony trials.

When I first made duck terrines I borrowed M.F.K. Fisher's recipe, and began to adjust the calls. In these days I had the energy and time to pare down dozens of breasts of pintail, and redhead and widgeon ad infinitum, struggling to reach the volume of birds needed to fill the terrines I was using. Eventually I learned that cold charcuterie is tricky work, and depends mostly on a strategic selection of spices. Farm-raised breasts have knocked the work in half, and protected my modest reserves of the wild ducks.

And if it's true that only hunters can savor a wood duck taken over pecans, there are also a great many city folks who savor the memory of Matt Garner's barbecue sauce over backyard duck, and swear to the heavens that there can be no higher art.

Garner ran a little place that got bigger as the night wore on. You might see the singer Lightnin' Hopkins, or the wild-catter Glenn McCarthy or the lawyer Percy Foreman scratchin' around for some place to sit.

"If you don't like my chairs, you can just bring your own," Matt Garner once said in his gruff but good-natured way to young Roy Hofheinz, who later became mayor of Houston.

From behind that crusted-over brick and cement pit he offered many sauces, but his best was a "finish" sauce. Not a marinade, or a slow-cooking flavor rub, a finish sauce has tomatoes and sugar and can only be brushed on ten minutes before serving. Otherwise it scorches and ruins both sauce and meat.

Slow cooking is as essential for pit-barbecue cooking of ribs and briskets as it is for ducks and geese. But in Chinatown, U.S.A. they have a slow/fast system that produces the lovely, long-necked, golden ducks hanging in the shop windows. This is the result of hours of steaming followed by a crackling hot ride in the frying pan or wok.

During the steaming process the hints of scallion and ginger creep into the meat, while the double frying brings the skin to a crackling crunch that is the pièce de résistance of spicy Szechuan cooking.

And through the range of all these, I cannot think of duck without gratitude to the many hunters and fancy chefs who have laid this table over hundreds of years. From Mr. Tom and his Teal in Clay Pot that warmed his 81 winters, to the exclamations of respect from my grandmother as she explained that the oyster and pecan stuffing brought good luck to the happy child who found the hidden oyster.

Ducks in their many forms are still flying high and fast, and the hunters on board "The Payson" are still squatting around a little brazier of red-hot coals as oysters pop open, and skeins of redheads buzz into the pink and blue sunset.

BRAISED DUCK BREASTS À LA JUS ORANGE

The sweet-tart orange flavors, accented by a tingle of peel, contrast the duck's mellow character. Whether your sauce accompanies a braised duck, and is called à la jus orange, or a roasted duck and is called a bigarade, the sauce must never be merely sweet.

2 whole duck breasts with skin, boned
Salt and pepper
5 carrots, peeled and split lengthwise
I tablespoon tomato paste
I cup veal stock
I cup Madeira
I tablespoon arrowroot

5 tablespoons unsweetened orange juice
3 tablespoons lemon juice
 (or 4 tablespoons Seville marmalade in place of
 orange and lemon juices)
2 tablespoons julienne of orange peel
I tablespoon julienne of lemon peel

Salt and pepper the duck breasts on both sides. On top of the stove, using a large sauté pan over medium heat, brown the breasts skin side down for 5 minutes, moving them around to avoid sticking. Pour off the excess fat that has cooked out from under the skin, turn the breasts and cook meat side down for 3 minutes. Remove the breasts and drain.

Parboil the carrots in salted water for 5 minutes, then remove and drain.

In a braising pan with a tight-fitting lid, soften the tomato paste in the veal stock over medium-high heat. Add half of the Madeira and whisk into the stock.

Introduce the duck breasts to this braising liquid skin side up. Cover, and set in a preheated oven at 375°F for 35 minutes. Baste the breasts several times. After 20 minutes add the parboiled carrots and continue to braise for an additional 15 minutes.

When the breast meat is resilient to the touch, and soft enough to cut with a spoon (at an internal temperature of about 145°F), remove the duck breasts and carrots to a warm platter and cover with foil.

In a small bowl, soften the arrowroot in the remaining Madeira. On top of the stove, add the arrowroot mixture to the braising liquid in the pan and reduce to a

(*Recipe continued on page 20.*)

Braised Duck Breasts à la Jus Orange (continued)

stiff consistency, about ½ cup. In a saucepan over very low heat slowly combine the reduced braising liquid with the orange and lemon juices (or the Seville marmalade) and simmer for 5 minutes, reducing slightly. Adjust the salt and pepper to taste. At the last minute add the julienne of orange and lemon peel, but do not allow the sauce to boil beyond this point.

Slice the duck breasts across the grain, and arrange the pieces on each serving plate. Serve the carrots, glaze the duck with the sauce, and send the balance of the jus orange to the table in a sauce boat.

CLAY POT TEAL ROAST IN PORT WINE SAUCE

With more land and more ducks than most people can imagine, Mr. Tom O'Connor kept it simple. Celery, wine and teal, blended to the magic of the simple clay pot.

I whole teal duck, cut up into 6 pieces
I lemon half
Salt and pepper
4 tablespoons fresh orange juice
I onion, thinly sliced

¼ teaspoon crushed red pepper
I teaspoon diced garlic
I celery stalk, trimmed and split in fourths
I cup port wine

Rub the lemon half over all the duck pieces then sprinkle with salt and pepper. Combine the orange juice, onion, red pepper and garlic in a large bowl or glass baking pan and marinate the duck parts for 4 hours, or overnight.

Soak the clay pot in water for 15 minutes. Drain the pot, and place the duck, marinade, celery and the wine in the pot. Cover.

Place the assembled pot in a cold oven, then set the temperature to 550°F. Bake for 30 minutes. Remove the lid and allow the pot to cook for another 5 minutes, or until the meat takes on some color.

Muscovy Breasts in Black Grape Sauce à la Vigneronne

Ripe black grapes bring a complexity to the sauce that belie its simple list of ingredients. When the duck and the grapes grow from the same soil in the same season all seems right.

2 whole duck breasts with skin, boned
2 tablespoons butter
2 tablespoons olive oil
Salt and pepper
1 cup thinly sliced onions
1 cup thinly sliced carrots
2 cups veal stock (or 3 tablespoons demi-glace)

2 cups black table grapes, puréed
5 tablespoons lemon juice
½ teaspoon crushed red pepper flakes
1 cup red wine (Merlot or other burgundy)
2 tablespoons butter, cut in small bits
1 cup black grapes, sliced in half

In a large sauté pan melt the butter and oil over medium-high heat. Salt and pepper the duck breasts, and brown them quickly, about 5 minutes per side. Remove the breasts to a warm plate, and in the remaining cooking oil soften the onions and carrots for 15 minutes, being careful not to brown the vegetables.

In a small saucepan reduce the veal stock to a glaze of 3 tablespoons over high heat. Meanwhile, when the carrots are soft enough to be crushed with a spoon, reduce the heat, and add the puréed grapes, lemon juice, red pepper and wine, and bring to a mild simmer. Add the reduced glaze to the simmering vegetables. Stir and allow to continue simmering for 20 minutes.

Remove the pan from the heat. Strain to remove seeds and skin, reserving the sauce. Return the sauce to the sauté pan. Add the duck breasts, ½ teaspoon of black pepper and braise the duck breasts over medium-high heat for 30 minutes.

Remove the duck breasts and keep warm. Reduce the sauce over high heat to a total of 2 cups. Over low heat whisk in the butter until the sauce begins to thicken. Add the sliced grapes and stir until they are warmed. Remove the sauce to pour over the breasts, sliced across the grain for serving.

GUMBO OF DUCK, COOT AND CRAB

If it doesn't have okra, you can't call it gumbo. But the more flavors, the more fun, so "laissez roulez les bons temps."

2 ducks, cut into serving pieces (8 pieces per duck)
2 coot, skinned and cut into serving pieces (or additional duck)
2 cups fresh lump crab meat, cooked
7 tablespoons butter, divided
2 cups fresh okra, trimmed and sliced
3 tablespoons flour
7 tablespoons olive oil, divided
½ cup chopped celery

2 cloves garlic, minced
1 green pepper, seeded and chopped
2 quarts water
3 bay leaves
1 tablespoon salt
2 dried red chili peppers
⅓ cup tomato paste
3 tablespoons filé powder (ground sassafras root), optional

In a 16-quart gumbo pot with a lid heat 4 tablespoons butter and sauté the okra. Lower the heat, add the flour and cook a few minutes until flour begins to brown, forming a roux.

Add 4 tablespoons olive oil, and stir in the celery, garlic and green pepper. Continue stirring another 3 minutes or so until the vegetables soften slightly.

Add the water, bay leaves, a teaspoon of salt, the chili peppers and tomato paste. Bring to a boil and let simmer 15 minutes while the meat is prepared.

In a separate skillet heat 3 tablespoons each butter and oil over medium-high heat, and brown each piece of duck and coot, adding them to the gumbo pot. Continue to simmer the gumbo with the duck and coot for an additional 30 minutes or until the meat is tender.

Add the crab meat and simmer for an additional 5 minutes. Turn off the heat and allow the gumbo to rest for 20 minutes. Spoon in the filé powder 5 minutes before serving. Taste and correct the seasoning, adding more salt if necessary.

PRESSED DUCK À LA TOUR D'ARGENT

In some circles it is considered the height of elegance to have the flying table rolled up beside your penthouse view of the Eiffel Tower while the subtle juices are sautéed down to a delicate flavor. The critical ingredients are a fresh, rare-cooked duck, and a dab hand at the sauté pan.

I whole duckling, young and plump
2 tablespoons lemon juice
½ cup Madeira
½ cup brandy (or less, to taste)

I cup duck consommé (or heavy veal stock)
Salt and pepper
I loaf duck press bread (*see recipe on page* 77)
A duck press and a double chafing dish

With a sharp knife trim away excess fat from the cavity of the bird. Rub the duckling with the lemon juice. Roast the duckling for not more than 20 minutes in a preheated oven at 450°F. (Pull the bird out of the oven at 17 minutes if you prefer the duck rare.)

Remove the breast skin and discard. Carve the breast meat off the bird. Slice the breasts lengthwise in four thin slices each, arranging the slices in a lightly buttered covered chafing dish over very low heat to keep warm during the preparation of the sauce. Carve away the legs and wings and send back to the oven for further roasting if they are to be served later.

On a cutting board, disassemble the bird's carcass using shears and place all the bones and bits in the press.

Sprinkle the Madeira over the bones, and press the contents to squeeze out all the blood and juices, returning them to a second warmed chafing dish. Add the brandy, and cook the sauce in the chafing dish without allowing it to boil, incorporating all the flavors by stirring gently. After 2 minutes add the consommé or stock, and stir continuously and long enough to reduce and thicken slightly, achieving a rich chocolate color.

The slices of breast meat should be well seasoned with salt and pepper, and placed on thin slices of duck press bread cut lengthwise from the loaf. The sauce is then spooned over the meat, and the combination served immediately. A good accompaniment is a watercress and walnut salad.

D'ARGENT

CANETONS

Le Caneton
Tour d'Argent

Le Caneton
Marco Polo
aux quatre
poivres

Le Caneton
Mazarine
aux
Oranges

Caneton Venaissin aux Olives
Caneton Bourdaloue à la Julienne de Citron
Caneton poivré Lavallière
Caneton d'au-delà les mers
à l'Ananas, aux Pamplemousses
Caneton aux quartiers de Pêches
Caneton de la Cerisaie
Caneton des Vendanges
Caneton Claude Foussier aux Pistaches
Caneton grillé aux Pommes de Reinette
Caneton Raphaël Weill
Caneton aux Huîtres
à la façon de M. A. Carême
Aiguillettes de Caneton
à la Gelée de Porto
(sur Commande)
Caneton en Terrine
des Yvelines
(sur Commande)

RÔTS

Poularde grillée Henry III

The Peking Roll with Red Cabbage and Sausage

Even back when the Peking Duck was known as a Long Island Duckling its splendid, crispy brown skin made it a buffet favorite.

1 whole duck (4 to 5 pounds)
1 head red cabbage
1 head fresh fennel
Salt and pepper
1 cup chopped onion
½ cup finely chopped serrano peppers (or green olives)

3 tablespoons butter
1 cup stale cornbread
2 anchovy fillets
⅓ cup sherry
1 egg, slightly beaten
1 pound link sausage, partly cooked

Remove the coarse outer leaves from the cabbage, core and discard the heart, and parboil the whole cabbage for 15 minutes. Rinse in cold water and drain. Remove the outside leaves and cut away the ribs at their bases. Separate the leaves and pat dry with paper towels.

Parboil the fennel in the same fashion (without coring), cooking for only 5 minutes to make the stalks malleable. Separate and pat dry.

Bone the duck from a midline incision down the backbone, separating the skin and meat still together from the carcass. Remove all leg bones, the wish bone (carved out delicately with a small knife), and the upper segment of the wing. Leave the bone at the tip of the wing in place. Lay out the skin and meat, meat side up, and salt and pepper the meat. Place the cabbage leaves and stalks of fennel over the duck in separate layers, about 3 leaves thick, reserving about 2 cups of cabbage and fennel.

Sauté the onions and peppers in the butter. In a food processor combine the softened onions, peppers, salt and pepper, corn bread, anchovies and remaining cabbage and fennel, including ends and bits, and whir until a uniform size is achieved. Moisten this mixture with the sherry and egg and whir briefly to form a forcemeat.

(*Recipe continued on page 30.*)

Close any large tears or holes in the duck skin, particularly the vent opening, using skewers and cotton twine. Spread the forcemeat evenly on top of the cabbage and fennel leaves, and stuff the leg and wing cavities with forcemeat to recreate a natural shape. Add the sausage arranged from head to toe on top of the forcemeat. Roll the bird from side to side to make an even larger, slightly overlapping sausage in the shape of the original duck. Secure the backline incision with poultry skewers and cotton twine. (*For further instructions on forming this ballotine, see procedure and illustrations on page 88.*)

In a preheated oven at 375°F roast the roll, breast side up, in an open roasting pan with the butter, basting frequently for 25 minutes. Turn the roll breast down and continue roasting for approximately 45 minutes, until the skin takes on a rich brown color. Turn the roll one last time, and continue roasting and basting to finish, about 15 minutes. The skin should be crispy brown. The roll is done when an internal temperature of 130°F is reached.

Remove and allow to cool. Remove the skewers and twine. Baste with the remaining juices and slice in ¾-inch rounds to serve.

DUCK SOUP WITH CONFIT DE CANNETON

All the legs of duck and goose brought into a kitchen should by some grand edict be immediately removed and consigned to confit.
The glorious outcome then graces soups, terrines, and pastas with a flavor that surpasses the roast thigh, and is the only just application of the second joint.

2 cups duck confit, thawed if frozen (*see recipe on page* 79)
1 leek, thinly sliced (or 1 cup sliced scallions)
1 carrot, thinly sliced
1 stalk celery with leaves, thinly sliced
½ cup Madeira
Salt and pepper

FOR THE STOCK:
2 duck carcasses (cooked or uncooked)
1 onion, coarsely chopped
1 carrot
1 stalk celery
9 cups water
Salt and pepper

To make 8 cups of duck stock, place the duck carcasses, onion, carrot and stalk of celery in a large pot with the water. Season lightly with salt and pepper and simmer very gently for 1 hour, skimming away any foam, until the bones separate and any remaining meat comes off easily.

Strain the stock into another pot, and add the sliced leek, carrot and celery and bring to a low boil for 20 minutes.

Wipe the confit clean of excess fat, cut into bite-sized pieces, and add to the stock and vegetables. Add the Madeira, adjust the seasonings and continue simmering for 10 minutes before serving.

Terrine à la Maison with Green Peppercorns

This duck terrine recipe started life in the kitchen of M.F.K. Fisher, but has spent the last twenty years at duck camps and picnics as its form gradually changed. You can change it again, so long as it is rich in fat and flavors, and served on a fresh linen napkin.

1½ cups skinned duck breast meat sliced in thirds
1 cup fresh ground pork fatback
1½ cups coarsely ground duck meat
1½ cups ground lean pork
½ cup ground lean veal
5 tablespoons butter, divided
⅓ cup finely chopped shallots (or scallions)
1 clove garlic, finely chopped
2 cups foie gras (or chicken livers soaked overnight in brandy), cut to spoon-size pieces
¼ cup Cognac

3 tablespoons heavy cream
2 teaspoons lemon juice
2 tablespoons flour
1 tablespoon pâté salt (*see recipe on page 80*)
1 egg, slightly beaten
1½ tablespoons salt
Freshly ground black pepper
¼ cup green peppercorns
1 large bay leaf for garnish
2 pounds pork fatback, sliced into ⅛-inch strips or sheets

Combine the ground pork fat, sliced duck breasts, ground duck meat, ground pork and ground veal in a large mixing bowl.

In a heavy 10-inch skillet, melt 3 tablespoons of butter over moderate heat. When the foam subsides, stir in the shallots and garlic and cook, stirring frequently, for 5 minutes, or until soft but not brown. With a spatula, scrape into the bowl of meat.

In the same skillet, melt 2 tablespoons of butter and cook the foie gras or chicken livers for up to 4 minutes, or until they are firm but still pink inside. Remove the livers with a slotted spoon and set them aside on a plate. Pour the Cognac into the hot skillet and boil, stirring and scraping any browned bits, until it has reduced to about 2 tablespoons. Pour this glaze over the meat and shallots. Set the skillet aside.

(*Recipe continued on page 34.*)

Add the cream, lemon juice, flour, pâté salt, egg, salt and a generous grinding of pepper to the meat mixture. Knead vigorously with both hands, then stir until the ingredients are well blended and the mixture is smooth and fluffy. Gently fold in the green peppercorns. Add more seasoning if desired. Preheat the oven to 350°F.

To prepare the mold, first lightly oil the inside and bottom of the terrine, then place a decorative bay leaf, shiny side down, flat in the center. Line the bottom and sides of the terrine with thin strips or sheets of pork fatback. Depending on their length, the strips may be arranged lengthwise or crosswise, but they should overlap slightly and completely cover the bottom and sides of the mold. If they are long enough, let them hang over the sides and later lap them back over the top of the filling; otherwise, save enough strips of the fat to cover the top of the terrine. (*See procedure on page 90*).

Spoon half of the meat mixture into the lined mold, pressing it down firmly and smoothing the top. Cut the foie gras or chicken livers into quarters or eighths, depending on their size, and lay them in a row down the center of the mold. Fill the mold with the remaining meat mixture. Smooth the top and bring the long strips of fat from the sides up over the meat or arrange additional strips over it. Enclose the top of the mold snugly with foil, then cover tightly with the lid. Place the mold in a large baking pan on the middle shelf of a preheated 350°F oven. Pour in enough boiling water in the pan to reach at least halfway up the side of the mold. Bake the terrine for up to 2 hours, or until the fat and juices that rise to the top are clear yellow.

Remove the terrine from the oven and lift off the cover and foil. Loosely cover the mold with fresh foil and weight the terrine with a casserole or cutting board weighing at least several pounds. Let cool, then refrigerate, with the weight still in place, until it is chilled.

To serve, first decant the terrine by placing the entire dish in a sink of very hot water (just deep enough to reach the sides of the terrine) for 10 minutes. Place a serving platter or carving board over the terrine and quickly invert the combination. The terrine will pop out onto the plate.

BREASTS OF DUCKLING WITH APPLES AND JUNIPER BERRIES

Store-bought ducks, Muscovy or Peking, even Nantes if they have it, are luscious enough to absorb the juniper and cider and bring good firm apples to the level of ambrosia.

2 whole duck breasts with skin, boned and halved
2 tablespoons olive oil
Salt and pepper
1 cup veal stock
1 cup nonpasteurized apple cider (or unsweetened apple juice)

2 tablespoons juniper berries, crushed
3 tablespoons butter, divided
1 tart yellow-skinned apple
1 tablespoon balsamic vinegar

In a large sauté pan bring the oil to medium heat. Season the breast halves with salt and pepper and cook slowly in the sauté pan, skin side down, until the fat is rendered and the skin takes on a rich, brown color. After 10 to 12 minutes turn the breasts and cook for 3 to 4 minutes.

Remove the breasts, pat dry, and reserve on a warm platter. Add the stock, cider and juniper berries to the sauté pan over high heat and reduce by half, scraping the pan all the while. Reduce the heat, whisk in 2 table-spoons butter and remove from heat. Allow the sauce to stand until needed, then strain and ladle over the duck when serving.

Peel, seed and thinly slice the apple into ten semi-circle pieces. In a sauté pan melt the remaining butter and add the vinegar. Heat through. Soften the apple pieces in the butter and vinegar mixture for 3 or 4 min-utes, until the apples are soft but not crumbling.

To serve, slice the breasts, arrange the apples beside each portion, and spoon the sauce over the duck and apples.

BACKYARD DUCK WITH DOWN-HOME SAUCE

Barnyard ducks are a well-guarded barbecue secret. The meat, always cooked slowly, is basted in its own fat,
succulent and full of mellow flavors, and then crisply finished with the crunch of a traditional barbecue.

4 whole breasts of Muscovy duck with skin, boned and
   halved
4 tablespoons olive oil
Salt and pepper

FOR THE SAUCE:
1 cup red wine vinegar
6 tablespoons brown sugar
½ teaspoon celery seed
½ teaspoon cayenne pepper (or more to taste)
1 teaspoon salt
1 tablespoon freshly cracked black pepper
2 tablespoons chopped garlic
2 tablespoons finely diced onion
1 cup Worcestershire sauce
4 tablespoons fine flour (or soy flour)
½ cup tomato paste
1 cup water
3 tablespoons lemon juice

Prepare the sauce the day before, or at least the morning before it is needed. In a small saucepan reduce the red wine vinegar over medium-high heat for 5 minutes. Add the sugar, celery seed, cayenne pepper, salt, black pepper, onion and chopped garlic and continue reducing until ½ cup of liquid remains.

In a bowl combine the Worcestershire sauce, flour, tomato paste and water until all the lumps are gone. Over a very low heat add the tomato mixture to the vinegar mixture, stir well, and continue to simmer for one hour. Taste for salt and gently stir in the lemon juice. Allow the sauce to stand at least 30 minutes before

(Recipe continued on page 38.)

using. Because this is a "finish" sauce and contains tomato and sugar it should be used during the final 5 to 10 minutes of barbecuing.

An hour and a half before you plan to eat, start the fire, and allow the coals to burn down for at least 30 minutes before cooking the duck breasts. Rub the duck breasts with the olive oil and liberally salt and pepper.

Over hot coals with no flame, place the birds on the grill not directly over the coals, skin side up for 15 minutes. Turn the birds and continue to grill for 10 minutes, then turn again for another 10 minutes, dousing any flames with water, until the birds are almost done.

Ten minutes before the breasts are done coat them with the sauce. At the final moment before serving, baste lightly once more, and, as the sauce reacts to the heat, remove the birds to a serving plate. Serve with pickles and tomatoes.

Canard Sauvage with Pecan and Oyster Stuffing

Of all my days in rough duck camps, this is the memory that comes back most often. Fresh oysters lift the dramatic tension, but the cornbread and sage anchor the experience.

4 mallard or pintail ducks, at least 4 pounds each
4 cups raw oysters, shucked and drained
Salt and pepper
2 onions, finely chopped
2 tablespoons olive oil
3 cups stale cornbread (*jalapeño-flavored optional, see recipe on page 80*)

1 cup broken pecans
¼ cup chopped parsley
½ teaspoon rubbed sage
½ cup duck stock (or less)
1 lemon, cut in 8 slices lengthwise

Salt and pepper each duck, inside and out, and set them all together on a rack in a large open roasting pan. In a sauté pan soften the onions in the olive oil.

Combine the onion, cornbread, pecans, parsley, sage and oysters, mixing carefully to distribute the oysters and the sage throughout, and then add just enough of the stock to soften the mixture only slightly. Stuff each duck with an equal portion. Place one lemon slice inside each duck on top of the stuffing, and reserve the others to garnish the serving plates.

In a preheated oven at 400°F roast the ducks, breast side up, basting every 10 minutes. Do not turn the ducks. They are done when an internal temperature of 150° is reached at the base of the thigh.

Remove the ducks when done, reserving the pan juices. Separate most of the fat from the pan juices, and reduce the juice quickly over high heat to serve with the ducks and oyster stuffing.

SZECHUAN DUCK BREASTS

*Farm-raised ducks are so endowed with fat and skin that the Chinese learned to make a virtue of it,
cooking the fat away at the same time as the skin gathered up the flavors of the ginger, soy and pepper.*

2 whole duck breasts with skin, boned
2 tablespoons salt
½ cup chopped scallions and tops
1 tablespoon ground star anise seeds
1 tablespoon crushed fresh ginger
2 tablespoons red pepper flakes, crushed

½ cup white wine
1 tablespoon soy sauce
1 tablespoon cornstarch
2 cups duck fat for frying (or vegetable oil)
Salt and pepper to taste.
Wei Hsion powder (or powdered star anise)

Rub the duck breasts with salt, then marinate in a bowl with the scallions, anise, ginger and pepper and wine sprinkled over. Place duck breasts, marinade and bowl in a steamer for 1 hour.

Remove duck breasts from the steamer, and scrape off the seasonings. Rub the breast skins with the soy sauce, and sprinkle with the cornstarch.

Fry the breasts in a deep vat of duck fat for 5 minutes at 375°F. Remove and drain. Fry the breasts again at 375°F for 10 minutes or until crispy.

Remove, drain and carve the breasts. Serve with extra salt and pepper and Wei Hsion powder, or powdered star anise, and applesauce Quebeçoise (*see recipe on page 81*).

"CHRISTMAS IS COMING

AND THE
GEESE ARE GETTING FAT . . ."

In most parts of the world the goose is many things to many people, but most certainly not a game bird to anyone. Throughout Europe and Asia domestic geese have waddled obligingly in farmyards for hundreds of years, and have become the stuff of gustatory legends.

Ask a German about the white Embden goose, and his eyes glaze over while thinking of rich braises with spaetzle dumplings. The French have created an industrial monopoly around goose liver, or foie gras, and the Chinese had geese so huge that Marco Polo came home bragging about them.

European geese flock conveniently together, weed the gardens, and grow fat on short rations of corn, waiting for Christmas. American honkers and specklebellies, on the other hand, came tumbling down through the quick low clouds. These are two very separate birds despite their taxonomical similarity, and, from a culinary point of view, two very separate dishes.

Raymond Camp, one of the most sensitive and dedicated cookers of migratory game, always picked a small goose at the back of the decoying flight when he knew the bird was destined for his own table. And what a treasure the young wild goose is on the table, with fine dark breast meat reminiscent of venison backstrap, and unique in its flavor.

The wild bird is lean and small, a first-year bird never weighs more than seven pounds, feathers and all, and comes to the table at something just under five pounds dressed. Its domestic cousin, born in May and after a summer of corn and weeds, feathers out to twenty pounds in the fall and reaches the kitchen at a promising ten to twelve pounds, oven ready.

There are, of course, stories of Canada Honkers so large that their wingspan blocked out the sun, and they weighed over twenty pounds when they hit the rice paddy. It seems I have been in on many of those hunts, and the joy of the hunters, back-slapping and bragging about the giant size, was itself a spectacle to behold. The mood changed as we neared the picking station, and, truth to tell, in a lifetime of hanging around cornfields and rice paddies from

Anáhuac to the Outer Banks I have never seen a true twenty-pound bird. And he would have been four years old and tough as a boot.

The bird from the sky is powerful and sagacious, a migratory marvel, but one that has to be coddled and carefully supported in the kitchen. The bird from the backyard, and increasingly available these days from the grocery store, is a bourgeois delight: fat, savory and adaptable to a full menu of choices.

The points of distinction between wild and tame are more than their similarities. For a roasted wild goose you must have a bird "of the year," and that means under seven pounds, feathered, with a pliable lower bill, and even in the biggest of wild birds that means negligible meat on the legs. The wild bird, roasted at 350°F, will present medium-rare breast meat of 150°F internal temperature if cooked at twelve minutes per pound. This is the supreme presentation of wild goose, and should be savored and sauced. Any wild bird of seven pounds or better is no baby, and should be breasted and braised slowly.

The tragedy of our diminishing wildlife resources is that some things, such as wild ducks and geese, aren't what they used to be in the flavor department. One example is the nutritional devastation to the Atlantic Brant population. This small, highly esteemed little goose had its whole East Coast diet yanked out from under it during the 1930s and '40s with the epizootic extinction of eelgrass. As a consequence the Brant of today feed off algae and other bare substitutes. The bird cascaded down the flavor scale from a gunner's delight to inedible status.

Another important difference is the fat content of the birds. The wild bird has none to speak of. The domestic bird, at five months of age, is rolling in fat that should be cooked or steamed away to satisfy contemporary notions of nutrition.

From a fashionable point of view, "goose for dinner" has been so decidedly "down market" for a hundred years that even Escoffier, usually a good sport willing to fry up lapwings and ortolans to please a king, sniffed at the prospect, "Apart from the foie gras, the preciousness of which is truly inestimable, goose is really only served at family tables."

But what jolly bourgeois tables they must have been and still are! The cassoulets, braises, and rich confits that the goose produces are the nourishing nursery food of millions of well-intended and happy people.

In these recipes I have made adjustments for modern sensibilities regarding the fat content in the domestic bird, and reduced the resulting fat through the use of ancient oriental methods, inscrutable and mysterious, such as steaming and browning. The wild birds, on the other hand, are helped along slightly with quick cooking in rich braising liquids calculated to reveal their brilliant flavor, and bring them up to par with their succulent domestic cousins. The wild birds simply cannot be substituted for domestic without adjusting the cooking times.

How the world of taste, fashion and perceived nutrition has come around from the time that a rich fat goose at Christmas was the apotheosis of a right world.

Christmas is coming,
And the geese are getting fat.
Please to place a penny in an old man's hat.
If you haven't got a penny,
A ha'penny will do
If you haven't got a ha'penny,
Then God bless you.

Before fear of food or fat was an issue, Tiny Tim and Bob Cratchit set high store by the crisp, roasted goose skin and the savory Yorkshire pudding that was popular at Christmas. The Yorkshire pudding recipe offered here is adapted from Jane Grigson, who reports her own fascination with the exploding fat and flour and the great crusty pudding that developed. Years later, beef crept into the Victorian diet, and it is a rich irony that current nutritional evaluations place the much-maligned duck and goose fat ahead of beef fat in the polyunsaturated sweepstakes.

The bourgeois appeal of goose is nowhere better demonstrated than in the cassoulet of the south of France. Julia Child herself goes on about it for six pages, and the crusty bread-crumb lid used here allows the various meat flavors to blend in a harmony that sweeps the ordinarily dour white beans into a frenzy of fine flavor.

This dish can theoretically be made with a wild bird, but requires more butter or oil to blend the flavor lines. The cassoulet of domestic goose promises complex bouquets caused by the mingling goose and fat and pork and sausage flavors, while the beans plod dutifully behind, slowly coming of age.

Which is the very effect the Cajun cook tries to bring to taste with his wild snow goose, but has to rely on the Maillard reaction so ably identified by Harold McGee. In this ordinary kitchen process, the browning giblets create color and flavor that enhance the sauce, and in turn the meat. Using young and old birds alike as one does in a country game kitchen, and as they come from the sky, the Cajun cook uses a slow, wet cooking procedure with a rich giblet gravy that gets its flavor from the meaty parts and seasonings, and lends succulence back to the sauce. This approach is also time honored in southern France, where rice and giblet gravy, without the rest of the bird, is a familiar tradition.

Good kitchen economy dictates that domestic goose and duck parts not served as an entrée are put by to become a rich "confit" to be used later in the year, whether in soups or terrines. And so it is always with great pleasure that I pull out a two-pound frozen package of confit to fill up a rough country terrine when I'm asked to bring something down to the hunting camp for the bears to maul over.

The Specklebelly Terrine offered here sits in any camp kitchen with pride, appealing by the broad stripe of its peppered bacon, and filled with hearty chunks of goose leg and thigh that have cooked and stewed in their own fat. Since it is a fact of every roast recipe that the leg joints don't cook at the same rate as the breasts it is practical to cut them out before hand for another use. This confit terrine can be eaten with Cumberland sauce, and jalapeño cornbread brought fresh from the oven.

The glorious goose in all its manifestations and with all its parts is also the ruling culinary art form in old Strasbourg. This happy bourgeois city is a never-never land where everything seems half French, half German, and part Swiss. They leave nothing to waste, and even make a sausage from the goose's neck. The fat skin has the effect of flavoring the chosen sausage mixture, in this case goose and pork, and hearty seasonings. This is one recipe where the American wildfowl hunter who picks his own birds is at an advantage; I have saved necks over a season from a variety of geese, and they work.

All over Strasbourg, and in fact throughout Alsace, gustatory peaks abound, protecting the good burghers from their neighbors' ambitions. There are exquisite local beers, including top fermenting ales, but no one thinks they are German. There is sauerkraut à l'alsacienne made here, but no one thinks it is foreign.

In the classless melting pot of America there are plenty of culinary celebrants who aren't afraid to appear bourgeois. Thirty years ago The Four Seasons Restaurant threw open its doors to an army of invading Hungarians to prove it. Every old Magyar warrior in the Manhattan telephone book came to a goose feast organized by Paul Kovi, the restaurant's owner. George Lang led the troops, which included James Beard and my pal Arie deZanger, presumably as neutral referees.

What they experienced was a cultural food bath of goose dishes, some recollected from childhood, some from memory or lore, but all in the whimsical spirit of soldiers abroad in a strange land, nostalgic for the plains of Hungary.

Some of the geese to be used in this potluck dinner were brought in by the guests, and to guard against any unwelcome surprises, and to protect the reputation of the great restaurant, Kovi used a fennel and fig recipe, rather like the one here, on all birds of suspicious provenance.

But all goose meat, even with the fat and skin removed, is still rich and provocative, and probably makes a better mousse than does pheasant. I once watched Maria Cuevas turn dark barnyard fowl into frothy, ornate incarnations of eggs and cream in a simple Mexican kitchen. No flowering mousse from the belle époque was more easily brought to hand with a sturdy whisk and copper bowl than was that goose in Cuernavaca, using techniques of metate and grinding stone as old as Mexican civilization.

Her kitchen looked out on the garden and over the garden wall northward from Cuernavaca toward the twin volcanoes of Ixtachehuatl and Cococapetl that guarded the Mexican capital. The mole sauce she preferred to use is based on the very modern dark sauces of the central mountain districts, but the commercial product is a reliable substitute.

A variation of this dish is made with the green mole and duck, called *Pato en Mole Verde de Pepitas,* using the self-same roasted pumpkin seeds that Aztecs chieftains were eating with their duck five hundred years ago when the first Spaniards arrived.

A hundred years after Cortez, chocolate and tomatoes, two of the enduring treasures form the New World, had worked their way into the game recipes of what is now the Basque country of northern Spain. One of those, brought home by Jane Grigson, I have happily adjusted for goose breasts.

But the goose knows his friends, and they are always from the old country. And as many ways as there are to sauce a German goose, the spaetzle, no matter which spelling you choose, steps into the role of sauce-bearer usually given to pasta in warmer climates. And the domestic Embden goose, cultivated for centuries all over Germany, steps onto the stage with an enormous presence at twenty pounds in its first year, rather like a Wagnerian tenor.

Once in Anchorage I was taking the tourist's peek through a high-tech kitchen presided over by a sturdy German chef, who was happily at home among his salmon pâtés and crab soufflés. We paused at one long shelf that contained colanders and ricers and graters, and in the corner were a collection of what he proudly described as his "spaetzle mills." I remember the shock of recognition when I realized that pride of place in the collection went to an ordinary 9 x 5 loaf pan with six bullet holes in the bottom.

"We were in the Brook's Range, and I had important friends from Baden," he said with a Teutonic nonchalance. "They wanted spaetzle with the sheep steaks! Don't you think it's a nice size?" He put a pencil through the holes, and smiled.

And that smile brought the goose around the world, loved and well fed, and providing for all. These recipes, including one from the ancient Chinese poet, Tai Pa, and another from the sturdy Minnesota pioneers, a potluck with wild goose and wild rice, demonstrate that with a slow hand in the cooking, goose has always been the nursery food of the civilized world.

CHRISTMAS ROAST GOOSE WITH YORKSHIRE PUDDING

Jane Grigson provided this Yorkshire pudding, and pointed out the traditional link with goose that pre-dates the popularity of roast beef. The golden crusted pudding is a reliable foil for rich goose gravy.

8- to 10-pound goose (domestic), giblets reserved
2 tablespoons olive oil
1 tablespoon butter
2 cups peeled and quartered onions
3 stalks celery, chopped
1 tablespoon salt
1 tablespoon freshly cracked black pepper
1 tablespoon dried sage
8 cups croutons — 1-inch cubes made from stale white
   bread with crust removed (or garlic croutons)
½ cup raw oysters, drained (optional)
½ cup goose stock
¼ cup Madeira (or less, optional)

FOR THE YORKSHIRE PUDDING:
4 eggs
1 teaspoon salt
½ teaspoon freshly cracked black pepper
½ teaspoon baking soda
1 cup milk
1 cup flour
4 tablespoons goose fat (or vegetable oil)

Both inside and out, rub the goose with 1 tablespoon of olive oil, and then some salt and pepper. Wrap the wing tips in aluminum foil to prevent scorching. With a sharp skewer or fork prick the skin of the bird under each leg and along a line below the breast for draining of the fat.

In a large skillet over medium heat soften the remaining olive oil and the butter. Sauté the onions and celery, being careful not to brown. After 5 minutes add the salt, pepper and sage. Stirring vigorously, continue sautéing over low heat for an additional 5 minutes.

Remove the skillet from the heat and stir in the croutons, and the oysters if used. When the mixture is well mixed moisten slightly with a bit of the stock, but not so much as to produce a wet stuffing. Stuff the

(Recipe continued on page 54.)

goose loosely with this mixture, and tie the feet together with a short length of kitchen string.

Add the remaining stock to a large roasting pan with a rack and supplement with enough water (and perhaps some Madeira for bouquet) for a total of 2 cups. Place the goose on the rack of the pan in an oven preheated to 375°F. Allow 20 minutes per pound cooking time for the domestic bird (which is medium to well done at an internal temperature of 170°F). Baste the bird several times with the pan juices.

After the goose is in the oven, start the Yorkshire pudding. Combine the eggs, salt, pepper, baking soda and milk in a processor and mix for 45 seconds. Allow the mixture to stand for 15 minutes and then slowly add the flour to the processor bowl, blending all the lumps away. Remove this batter to a mixing bowl and refrigerate for an hour, or until needed thereafter.

When the goose is done, remove from the oven, and place covered on a warmed serving platter for 30 minutes before removing the strings and carving.

Reserve 3 to 4 tablespoons of the goose fat from the roasting pan for the Yorkshire pudding. In a small roasting pan, heat the goose fat in an oven preheated to 450°F until the fat crackles, but does not smoke. Re-mix the batter briefly with a whisk and then quickly pour the entire batter into the hot pan, and return it immediately to the 450°F oven for 20 minutes. Watch the pudding carefully to avoid scorching, and cover loosely with aluminum foil after 10 minutes if necessary. The Yorkshire pudding is done when it climbs the edges of the pan unevenly and has a golden brown crust.

Carve the goose (*see procedure on page 84*) and spoon out crusty servings of Yorkshire pudding on each plate. Serve with giblet gravy and applesauce Quebeçoise (*see recipes on page 81*).

POACHED GOOSE BREASTS WITH ROASTED GARLIC CREAM SAUCE

Goose breasts carefully lifted from wild birds can be supported in this poaching process to avoid drying, and allowed to draw richness from the roast garlic and cream.

4 goose breast halves with skin, boned
1 head of garlic
2 tablespoons olive oil
Salt and pepper
1 teaspoon marjoram

1 cup plus 1 tablespoon dry sherry, divided
1 cup heavy cream
¼ teaspoon cayenne pepper
1 tablespoon arrowroot
½ cup fresh parsley, chopped

Rub an entire head of garlic, paper and all, with a bit of the olive oil, and place in an open roasting pan. Bake in the oven for 30 minutes at 300°F. Remove and allow to cool.

In a large sauté pan over medium heat warm the remaining oil. Cook the goose breasts all at once, skin side down, moving them around with a spatula to avoid sticking or scorching. Turn the meat after 4 minutes. Turn once or twice more until uniformly browned on both sides, and the skin has lost most of its fat.

Remove the meat to a warm platter. Season with the salt, pepper, and marjoram. Pour off most of the cooking fat, leaving enough to cover the bottom of the pan.

Return the seasoned meat to the pan, add a cup of sherry, and over very low heat poach the meat, covered, for 20 minutes. They are finished at an internal temperature of 150°F, or when the juices run clear. Remove the goose pieces to a warm platter.

Pop each clove of garlic out of the paper shells. In a processor purée the garlic, adding the cream and cayenne pepper. Reserve. Mix the arrowroot with a tablespoon of sherry and reserve.

Reduce the remaining pan juices to a few tablespoons of frothy essence over high heat, scraping any loose bits from the bottom and sides. Reduce the heat to low, add the garlic cream mixture and allow to boil slightly. Continue stirring and add the arrowroot mixture, warming the sauce until it thickens. Carefully add salt and pepper to taste, and return the goose pieces to warm in the sauce. Serve with the parsley sprinkled over.

Cassoulet de Toulouse with White Beans

This is the crusty bean pot simmering away for hours on end at the back of the stove that is the stuff of the legend of Provence.
Goose, pork and beans dance together in a timeless quadrille that can be balanced with a dark-crumbed bread to bring out a reliable crust.

7 cups goose meat, skinned, boned, and cut into 2-inch pieces
¼ cup flour
Olive oil for browning
2 cups onion sliced into thin rings
4 cloves garlic, mashed
2 tablespoons tomato paste
½ teaspoon thyme
2 bay leaves
3 cups dry vermouth (or dry white wine)
6 cups goose stock (or veal or brown stock)
2 cups raw spicy link sausage, split in half and cut into 2-inch pieces
3 cups dry white bread crumbs (or duck press bread crumbs, *see recipe on page* 77) mixed with ½ cup chopped parsley
2 Dutch ovens (or casseroles), one 8-quart and one 6-quart

FOR THE BEANS:
2 cups dry white beans (Great Northern or navy)
2 quarts water
1 cup chopped onions
4 garlic cloves, unpeeled
8 parsley sprigs
2 cloves
½ teaspoon thyme
4 bay leaves
Salt and pepper

First, prepare the beans. Bring the water to a boil in the large Dutch oven. Drop the beans into the boiling water. Boil for 5 minutes. Remove from the heat and let the beans soak in the water for an hour.

Place the onions, garlic, parsley, cloves, thyme and bay leaves in the large Dutch oven with the beans and water. Bring to a simmer. Skim off any foam and scum. (*Recipe continued on page 58.*)

Simmer slowly, uncovered, for 1½ hours, until the beans are tender. Add boiling water if necessary during cooking to keep beans covered with liquid. Season to taste near the end of cooking. Remove from heat and allow beans to rest in the cooking liquid. Drain and reserve the bean cooking liquid and the beans separately.

Now prepare the rest of the cassoulet. Dredge the goose meat lightly in the flour. In the smaller casserole on top of the stove, brown the goose meat in a little olive oil over medium-high heat, a few pieces at a time, on all sides.

Remove the meat as it is browned to a dish. If the oil burns discard it and add fresh olive oil. After all the meat is browned, soften the onion slices in the same casserole in olive oil over low heat for about 5 minutes. Remove the onion from the pan, reserving the cooking oil. Return the goose meat to the casserole, add the garlic, tomato paste, thyme, bay leaves, vermouth and stock. Simmer for an hour and a half, loosely covered. Strain the liquid and reserve the meat and the liquid separately.

In the larger Dutch oven spread half the beans in a layer across the bottom, then add all the goose meat and the sausage slices. Cover with the remainder of the beans. Pour on the reserved meat cooking juices, and enough bean cooking juice so the liquid just covers the top layer of beans. Spread 2 cups of the bread crumbs on top, and dribble the reserved cooking oil over all.

Preheat the oven to 375°F. Bring the casserole to a simmer on top of the stove, then set the uncovered casserole in the upper half of the oven. When the top has crusted lightly, after about 20 minutes, turn the oven down to 350° and cook for an hour and a half. Watch the cooking to prevent scorching.

Occasionally break the forming crust with the back of a spoon, and baste with additional bean cooking liquid. Repeat several times, as the crust re-forms, but leave a final crust intact for serving. Sprinkle with the remaining bread crumbs for the final browning. The finished cassoulet should have an attractive red and brown crust. Remove from the oven and allow it to rest before serving directly from the casserole.

Tai Pa Goose with Sweet and Sour Sauce

Venerable Chinese poets liked their goose, and they liked their wine. This process reduces the fat, and leaves the bird freshly braced up by the scallion and ginger.

1 whole 18-pound goose
1 cup white wine
4 scallions with tops, chopped
4 slices ginger
2 tablespoons soy sauce
1 teaspoon salt
2 tablespoons brown sugar

FOR THE SWEET AND SOUR SAUCE:
1 cup chicken stock (or less)
¼ teaspoon salt
½ cup sugar
½ cup cider vinegar
1 tablespoon soy sauce
½ cup pineapple juice
2 tablespoons arrowroot
¼ teaspoon ground cayenne pepper
2 tablespoons rice wine

Bring a 16-quart stock pot half full of water to a boil and place the goose into the boiling water for 15 minutes. Remove the goose and drain, then place the goose in a shallow bowl just large enough to contain the bird. Add the wine, scallions, ginger, soy sauce, salt and sugar to the bottom of the bowl.

Cover the bowl with aluminum foil and place the foil-wrapped bowl in a steamer, or on a rack in a large roasting pan with an inch of water. Steam for 2 hours. Remove the scallions and ginger and reserve the liquid in the bowl.

To make the sauce, transfer the liquid from the steaming bowl to a saucepan and add enough stock to total 1 cup of liquid. Add the salt, sugar, vinegar, soy sauce and pineapple juice and bring the contents to a boil. Mix the arrowroot and cayenne pepper into the rice wine, then add this to the saucepan. Reduce the heat, and allow to thicken for 3 minutes at a slow simmer. Carve the bird into serving sections and serve at once with the sweet and sour sauce.

Cajun Snow Goose with Dirty Rice and Giblets

The browning of the giblets, peppers, and onion produces a brown gravy that flavors and colors the rice during cooking. Cajuns don't traditionally use sherry in their cooking, but I never knew one who would turn it down.

1 snow goose cut into 8 pieces, giblets reserved
4 tablespoons rendered goose fat (or vegetable oil)
2 cups peeled and coarsely chopped onions
1 large green pepper, stemmed, seeded and coarsely chopped
2 cups goose giblets (or chicken giblets), finely chopped
½ cup coarsely chopped celery
2 tablespoons olive oil
1½ teaspoons salt

½ teaspoon freshly ground black pepper
1 teaspoon crushed red pepper
1 garlic clove, diced
1 tablespoon bouquet garni
4 cups goose stock (or veal stock or water)
1 cup uncooked basmati rice
½ cup dry sherry
½ cup finely chopped fresh parsley
Filé powder (ground sassafras root), optional

In a sauté pan over medium heat, thoroughly brown each piece of goose in the fat for 10 minutes. Remove the meat and set aside, reserving the fat. Soften the onions and green pepper in the reserved fat.

Purée the giblets, celery, onions and green pepper in a processor for 2 minutes, adding slight amounts of the reserved fat if necessary to speed the mixing.

In a heavy 4- or 5-quart casserole, heat the olive oil over moderate heat. Add the ground giblets and onion mixture and any remaining fat. Stir in the salt, black pepper, red pepper, garlic and bouquet garni, and reduce the heat to low. Stirring occasionally, cook uncovered for about 10 minutes, or until the meat is richly browned.

Add half the stock, the rice and goose meat and simmer over low heat, covered, for an additional 30 minutes.

Add the sherry, and stir once. Remove the casserole from the heat and allow it to rest 10 minutes, still covered, before serving. (The liquid remaining in the pot is served with the rice.)

Taste for seasoning and stir in the parsley. Ladle the dirty rice and cooking liquid into a shallow soup bowl and add a few pieces of goose on top. At the table offer a small bowl of filé powder for a sprinkling of flavor contrast.

Specklebelly Terrine with Pistachios

If you have saved enough goose and duck legs as confit you may make this entirely a goose leg terrine. In any event, the hearty slice will stand up to any good tailgate mayonnaise.

2 cups goose breasts sliced into 1-inch strips
3 cups cooked goose confit (*see recipe on page* 79)
1 cup raw pork chops with fat cut into 2-inch cubes
1 clove garlic, minced
1 teaspoon dried thyme
1 teaspoon dried rosemary
1 teaspoon salt
1 tablespoon crushed red pepper (optional)

1 teaspoon pepper
⅓ cup dry sherry
¼ cup Cognac
1 bay leaf
1 pound fresh bacon (or pepper bacon)
1 egg, slightly beaten
4 tablespoons chopped fresh parsley
1 cup pistachio nuts, roughly chopped

In a bowl combine the garlic, thyme, rosemary, salt, peppers, sherry, goose confit and cubed pork. Stir to coat. In another bowl combine the goose breast strips and the Cognac and set aside to marinate for 1 hour.

Place a nice bay leaf on the bottom a terrine or loaf pan. Then line the pan with strips of bacon, laying them across the bottom and the sides slightly overlapping. Select two or three slices of bacon to line the ends of the terrine. In all the bacon should overlap the edges and dangle down sufficiently to eventually fold back over the assembled terrine.

Drain any excess marinade from the confit and pork mixture and reserve. In a processor chop the confit and pork mixture to a medium consistency, adding the egg and parsley and a drop of the marinade to keep the mixture moving, forming a forcemeat. Remove the goose breasts from the Cognac and drain.

Pack half the processed forcemeat into the prepared pan. Sprinkle half the nuts over the forcemeat, then arrange half of the sliced goose breasts in a single layer. Complete the terrine with the second half of the forcemeat, the remaining nuts and finally the remaining goose.

(*Recipe continued on page 64.*)

Fold the bacon slices up and over the top, and add additional bacon to cover any gaps.

Cover the loaf loosely with aluminum foil, and place the pan in a larger baking pan. Add 1 inch of boiling water and bake in an oven preheated to 350° for up to 2 hours, or until the fat and juices run clear. Remove the loaf pan from the oven and allow to cool for 1 hour. Place a weight, such as a brick wrapped in foil, over the terrine and refrigerate overnight. To serve, decant the entire terrine on a platter, with the bay leaf now on the top of the terrine, and make generous serving cuts. Serve with Cumberland sauce (*see recipe on page 79*).

Goose Breasts al estilo Basque

*Practically the first boat back from the Americas brought tomatoes and chocolate to the coast of northern Spain,
where the wily indigenous chefs lost no time in fashioning a recipe for their local favorite, the goose.*

2 goose breast halves, bone in
2 each, goose legs and thighs
2 tablespoons olive oil
1 cup sliced onions
½ cup thinly sliced carrots
1 cup chopped skinned tomatoes
2 garlic cloves, crushed
4 tablespoons chopped parsley, divided

1 cup goose stock (or water)
½ teaspoon grated nutmeg
1 tablespoon red wine vinegar
Salt and pepper
5 teaspoons grated unsweetened baking chocolate
¼ cup dry sherry
½ teaspoon lemon zest (optional)

Brown the goose breast and leg parts in the olive oil, allowing the fat to drain from the goose skin without burning. Remove the meat to a casserole, placing the breast skin side down and the jointed legs alongside. Add the onions, carrots, tomatoes, garlic and 2 tablespoons chopped parsley to the casserole around the edges. Blend the nutmeg and vinegar into the stock, and pour over the meat and vegetables, adding enough stock or water to nearly cover the meat. Salt and pepper to taste.

On top of the stove bring the casserole to a low simmer, cover, and continue cooking for 25 minutes, until the goose breasts are tender. Remove the meat to a warm platter and reserve the cooking liquid for the sauce. Place all the cooking liquid and vegetables in a processor and purée for 1 minute, in two batches if necessary. Strain 2 cups of this mixture back into a saucepan, add the chocolate and the sherry and simmer for 10 minutes over very low heat. Taste for seasoning. Add a touch of lemon zest if desired.

To serve, carve the breast meat from the bone, and slice each breast in transverse sections and arrange on plates, surrounded by the whole legs and thighs. Ladle the sauce over. Serve with buttered noodles or spaetzle and sprigs of parsley scattered generously over all.

Goose-neck Sausage with Sauerkraut and Beer

Older than America, this sturdy peasant application of the obvious sausage casing left over from every hunter's sport afield will enrich any sausage recipe. The crisping of the sausage skin is a bonus, making this a link improved by the backyard grill.

5 goose necks with skin, picked clean
1 cup fresh goose livers and giblets, finely chopped
   (or chicken livers)
5 cups lean ground turkey sausage (or ground lean pork)
1 cup finely chopped onions
½ teaspoon olive oil
½ cup chopped parsley
1 teaspoon rubbed sage

1 teaspoon ground cayenne pepper
Salt and pepper
1 teaspoon ground cloves
1 teaspoon ground nutmeg
1 cup bread crumbs
2 eggs, beaten
½ cup rendered goose fat

Carefully peel the skin off each goose neck, leaving the tube of skin intact for stuffing. (Discard the meat and bones of the necks.)

Sauté the onions in olive oil until soft but not brown. In a large mixing bowl, combine the livers, ground turkey sausage, onions, parsley, sage, cayenne, salt, pepper, cloves, nutmeg and bread crumbs with the beaten eggs. Pack the stuffing into the neck skins, about 1½ cups per skin.

With cotton string tie the ends of the skins closed, then pierce the skins with the point of a sharp knife in several places. Preheat the oven to 375°F. In an open roasting pan, roast the sausages in the fat, basting and turning to prevent burning, for 50 minutes or more until well browned and crisp.

Remove from the heat and allow to cool slightly. Discard the string and slice the sausages in serving-size pieces, arranging them on a plate with sauerkraut with caraway seeds. Serve with salt and a crust of bread.

FOOD AND WIN...

A Traditional Hungarian Goose ...

THE THIRTY-FIRST OF MARCH

NINETEEN HUNDRED AND SEVENTY

THE FOUR SEASONS
NEW YORK

Wild Maygar Goose Braised with Figs and Fennel

With the irrepressible George Lang leading the charge, the luscious fruit flavors propel the rich goose tastes and scents to the foreground. This goose must be enjoyed in the bold Hungarian way.

1 wild goose (or domestic goose)
1 cup dried figs
1 cup Madeira
2 tablespoons olive oil
2 tablespoons butter
1 small onion, sliced
1 head of fennel, trimmed, cored, and thinly sliced

Salt and pepper
1⅓ cups stock (veal or other)
½ teaspoon mace
2 teaspoons lemon juice
1 tablespoon butter, shaved into bits
1 cup lightly chopped fennel leaves for garnish

Split the figs in half and set to marinate in a small bowl with the Madeira.

In a skillet, warm the olive oil and butter and sauté the onions and fennel slices until soft, but not brown. Salt and pepper the goose inside and out, and stuff with the onion and fennel mixture (including the oil and butter) and place breast side up in a braising pot with a tight-fitting lid. Pour ⅓ cup of stock in the pot, bring to a simmer on top of the stove, then cover and place in a preheated 350°F oven for 30 minutes.

Remove the bird from the braising pan, and pour off the accumulated fat, leaving the cooking juices in the pan. Return the bird to the braising pan, breast side up. Add the remaining cup of stock, the figs and the Madeira, and sprinkle the breast of the bird with the mace. Return the braising pan, uncovered, to the 350°F oven for 20 minutes, or until the skin develops a nice brown color.

Remove the bird to a carving board and allow to rest. Strain the cooking liquid, removing the figs to a serving platter. To the strained sauce add the lemon juice and shaved butter bits, heating slightly and allowing the sauce to thicken.

To serve, carve the breasts off the bird, and then carve each breast in thin transverse slices. Top with the fennel leaves, figs and the braising sauce.

Ganso Formidable — Goose Mousse with Mole

Before Columbus' arrival the Aztecs ate waterfowl with a mole sauce pounded out on stone grinders called molcajetes.
In this recipe for a buffet appetizer, the food processor spins out an airy mousse that the old lava rock utensils could not achieve,
with a hardtack cracker that could have made the ride down from Dolores Hidalgo in Pancho Villa's saddlebags.

2 cups raw, skinned goose meat, with sinew, fat, and gristle removed
2 tablespoons lemon juice
½ teaspoon white pepper
½ teaspoon salt
½ teaspoon pâté salt (*see recipe on page 80*)

2 egg whites, slightly beaten
1 cup heavy cream
2 cups mole sauce from concentrate
⅓ cup broken pecans
3 tablespoons finely chopped scallion tops
4-cup mold, buttered

Combine the goose, lemon juice, white pepper, salt and pâté salt in a processor bowl and whir for 2 minutes. With the machine whirring, add the egg whites and continue processing until uniformly blended. Remove the mixture from the processor to a small bowl, and refrigerate for 2 hours.

Place the cream in a cleaned processor bowl and whir for half a minute, (until the cream begins to take on body).

Add ⅓ cup of the beaten cream and 1 tablespoon of the mole sauce to the refrigerated meat mixture, and combine it carefully with a spatula.

In the processor whir the remaining ⅔ cup of cream to stiff peaks, then paddle it carefully into the meat mixture. Add the pecans and scallions to the mousse in the same fashion, and fold the mousse into the buttered mold.

Cook the mousse in a bain marie, covered, in an oven preheated to 350°F for approximately 1 hour, or until the mixture has set. Remove from the oven and allow the mousse to cool for at least an hour before decanting and serving. Turn out onto a large platter and spoon the remaining warm mole sauce in a bath over the mousse, covering the top and allowing it to drip down the sides. Serve with a basket of Pancho Villa's hardtack (*see recipe on page 78*) or fresh crackers.

BRAISED BREASTS OF EMBDEN GOOSE WITH SPAETZLE

Grand meals in the bourgeoisie tradition have a ritual air, setting goose against dumpling, as it has ever been at grandmother's table. This dumpling is called spaetzle, and the smaller and lighter the better, like pasta, to produce more surface area to carry more sauce.

2 whole goose breasts with skin, boned
3 tablespoons olive oil
2 small onions, sliced
4 carrots, split and halved
¼ teaspoon sage
¼ teaspoon thyme
½ tablespoon lemon zest in fine threads
1 cup Madeira
1 cup veal stock (or goose stock)
3 tablespoons arrowroot

FOR THE SPAETZLE:
2 cups white flour
3 eggs, slightly beaten
1 teaspoon salt
½ teaspoon nutmeg
⅓ cup water
1 tablespoon fresh rosemary, chopped (or fresh parsley)
1 tablespoon vegetable oil
4 tablespoons butter

In a skillet, brown the breasts in the olive oil skin side down, turning once or twice to avoid sticking. Add more olive oil if necessary after the goose fat has rendered out from under the skin, but continue browning until the skin takes on a golden hue, and the meat is colored.

Remove the breasts, drain, and place skin side up in a braising pot large enough to hold all breasts in a single layer.

In the same skillet over low heat, soften the onions and carrots in the remaining goose fat. Sauté for 10 minutes without browning. With a slotted spoon remove the onions and carrots and spoon them around the goose in the braising pot. Add the sage and thyme, and carefully sprinkle the threads of lemon peel along the top of the goose breasts. Add the Madeira and stock and bring the mixture to a simmer on the top of the stove.

(*Recipe continued on page 74.*)

Place the covered braising pot in an oven preheated to 375° F and cook for 20 minutes. Raise the temperature to 400°F, remove the lid and continue cooking the goose, basting occasionally until done, about another 20 minutes (or to an internal temperature of 180°F). Strain the cooking liquid, discarding the onions and reserving the carrots. Add 3 tablespoons of arrowroot to the liquid, and heat gently to thicken. Save this sauce for final assembly.

After the braising pot goes into the oven you can begin the spaetzle. In a mixing bowl, combine the flour, eggs salt, nutmeg and water and stir vigorously for 5 minutes. When the flour forms a paste, and small bubbles rise when resting, it is ready. Stir in the rosemary.

In a large pot, bring 2 quarts of water to a hard boil. Select a colander or spaetzle mill that can rest on the lip of the pot, and leave 2 inches of clearance above the boiling water. Add the vegetable oil to the water.

Pour the paste, all at once if possible, into the colander or spaetzle mill, and using a spatula force the dough through the holes (the holes should be between ¼ and ⅜ of an inch in size). Allow the spaetzle to cook for 2 minutes; it will rise to the top when done. Allow to boil another 30 seconds if the pieces are thick, then drain immediately.

Place the drained spaetzle in a cold water bath or under running water until thoroughly cooled. Drain off all water and reserve for final assembly.

Immediately prior to serving, melt the butter in a large skillet over medium heat. As the butter begins to brown add the spaetzle and toss quickly to coat.

Spoon the warm spaetzle onto platters, add the goose breasts and carrots, and cover with the thickened gravy. Serve with cold apple cider and applesauce Quebeçoise (*see recipe on page 81*).

North Woods Skidgeroo — Goose and Wild Rice Casserole

From Paul Bunyan to the present the North Woods boys and girls want it all in one easy pot luck dish.
Wild rice is so compatible with this process, and is never exacting about its liquid requirements, as long as there is plenty. And the better the stock the better the skidgeroo.

2 cups goose meat cut in bite-sized pieces, bones and
   tendons removed
Salt and pepper
3 tablespoons flour
2 tablespoons olive oil
I cup uncooked wild rice, rinsed

2 cups veal stock
2 tablespoons butter
I cup sliced fresh mushrooms
I cup fresh raw turnips, peeled and cut in small cubes
I garlic clove, peeled and chopped
½ cup sliced water chestnuts, drained

Salt and pepper the goose meat, then dust with the flour. In a skillet over high heat bring the oil to almost smoking and toss in the goose all at once. Toss the meat while cooking to avoid sticking. Remove from the heat after the meat begins to color and reserve the cooking fat.

In the meantime, combine the wild rice, ½ teaspoon salt and stock in a pot and quickly bring to a boil. Stir, reduce the heat and cover, simmering for 30 minutes.

Add the butter to the reserved fat in the skillet. Over low heat, add the mushrooms, I teaspoon each of salt and pepper, and soften for 5 minutes. Add the turnips and garlic and continue softening for 2 minutes more. Add the goose meat and the water chestnuts, remove from the fire, and allow the meat to warm in the skillet.

Rub scant olive oil around the inside of a I½-quart casserole. Pour in the warm goose mixture, and then all of the wild rice and stock over that. In an oven preheated to 350°F bake the casserole covered for 30 minutes, then uncovered for an additional 20 minutes, until the liquid has reduced to the level of the meat and rice, and a crust is forming. Serve using a slotted spoon onto individual plates with a slice of jalapeño cornbread *(see recipe on page 80)*.

SUPPORTING RECIPES

DUCK PRESS BREAD

3½ cups whole wheat flour, divided
2½ teaspoons yeast
1 teaspoon salt
2½ cups buttermilk

⅓ cup molasses
1 tablespoon powdered wheat gluten
½ cup rye flour
2 tablespoons butter, diced and frozen

Begin by making a liquid yeast starter: Into a large bowl add 1 cup of whole wheat flour, 1¼ teaspoons of yeast, 1 teaspoon of salt, and 1½ cups of the buttermilk. Then add ⅓ cup of molasses heated to a tepid stage, and 1 tablespoon of wheat gluten. Stir thoroughly and allow to bubble in a warm (85°F+) draft-free environment for 2 hours.

In a processor bowl combine the starter, rye flour, chilled butter bits, and the remaining yeast and buttermilk. Blend thoroughly. Add the remaining whole wheat flour and process, until you have a wet, sticky dough that adheres loosely to itself.

Turn the dough out onto a working surface, and using a pastry shovel continue to work the dough for a 20-count, incorporating scant dry four as needed to form a very loose, sticky dough. Place the dough in a covered dish and allow to rise until doubled in volume, about 2 to 3 hours, in a cool (72°F) environment. (If necessary, you may freeze the dough overnight after this first rising.) Knead the dough and allow to rise a second time, covered, for 2 hours in a cool environment.

Knead the dough again, form a loaf shape and fold the ends in. Allow to rise a final time in an oiled loaf pan (or pullman pan). This recipe is enough for a 9 x 5 loaf pan. The dough should fill half of the greased pan, and should fill about ⅔ of the loaf pan after rising.

Cover the pan with oiled aluminum foil. Then place a cookie sheet over the foil, and a 5-pound weight on top of the cookie sheet to force the compacting of the crumb. Bake for 35 minutes at 425°F. Remove the foil, baking sheet and weight, and allow the crust to brown slightly for 5 minutes. Remove from the oven and allow to cool. Remove the bread from the pan and allow it to rest for several hours. Wrap tightly until needed. The loaf can be refrigerated or frozen.

Pancho Villa's Hardtack

¼ cup canola oil
2 tablespoons butter
¾ cup milk
1½ cups all-purpose flour
1 cup cornmeal

2 teaspoons salt
2 teaspoons ground cumin
½ teaspoon baking soda
2 tablespoons whole cumin seeds (optional)

In a small bowl blend the oil and butter until smooth. Add the milk and mix thoroughly. In a large bowl combine the flour, cornmeal, salt, ground cumin and soda. Mix well.

Pour the oil mixture into the flour and combine with a spatula, incorporating all into a very thick dough. Refrigerate for 30 minutes.

This mixture is enough to cover two baking sheets, so divide the dough in half and return one half to the refrigerator. On an oiled baking sheet roll out half the dough with a heavily floured rolling pin. Tears should be patched. Keep the rolling pin floured while rolling out the thinnest possible dough, about ⅛ inch, filling the entire sheet. Sprinkle the cumin seeds across the surface of the dough if desired, and finish with one light pass of the rolling pin.

Use the tines of a fork to prick the dough at 2-inch intervals. Use a serrated cutter to score the individual crackers, about 2 x 4 inches. The crackers will separate during cooking.

In a preheated 325°F oven place the baking sheet in the center and bake for 15 minutes. Watch the crackers for signs of coloring and take them out before they scorch. The crackers can be turned after 15 minutes, and may be cooked for an additional 5 minutes on the underside.

Remove the crackers to a cooling rack, clean and re-oil the baking sheet, and repeat the process with the remaining half of the dough. Makes a total of about 24 crackers.

CUMBERLAND SAUCE

1 tablespoon onion pulp
3 tablespoons red wine vinegar
½ teaspoon arrowroot
3 tablespoons red currant jelly
2 tablespoons orange juice

1 tablespoon orange zest
1 tablespoon lemon zest
1 tablespoon prepared mustard
1 tablespoon port wine
½ teaspoon cayenne pepper

Simmer the onion and vinegar together in a small saucepan for 2 minutes. Add the arrowroot, jelly, juice and zests and continue simmering for an additional 2 minutes. Remove from the heat, and stir in the mustard, wine and cayenne thoroughly. Refrigerate for 2 hours before serving.

CONFIT OF DUCK OR GOOSE

3 cups duck or goose meat, skinned and boned
1 tablespoon salt
½ teaspoon thyme
¼ teaspoon freshly cracked black pepper

1 tablespoon pâté salt (*see recipe on page 80*)
¼ teaspoon ground red pepper
2 cups rendered duck or goose fat (or equal parts canola oil and fat)

In a small bowl combine the meat with the salt, thyme, black pepper, pâté salt and red pepper. Mix thoroughly and allow to stand overnight.

In a heavy skillet bring the fat to a boil, then reduce to a simmer. Add the meat and continue cooking over low heat for 1 hour. When the meat is done there will be no juice when the meat is pricked with the tip of a sharp knife.

Remove the skillet from the heat and allow to cool. In a sterilized bowl pack the meat carefully, then pour the fat over. If necessary, weight the meat down to keep it from floating. When the meat and fat are cool remove to the freezer. This mixture will keep for months. To use, defrost and wipe the fat away from the meat.

Jalapeño Cornbread

1 cup ground yellow cornmeal
1 cup all-purpose flour
2 teaspoons baking soda
½ teaspoon salt
½ teaspoon freshly cracked black pepper

1 cup milk
1 egg, slightly beaten
¼ cup vegetable oil (or duck fat)
½ cup pickled jalapeño peppers, drained and chopped

Preheat the oven to 400°F. Oil a 9-inch mold or baking pan. (If using a mold it may be helpful to heat it to cooking temperature before introducing the batter.)

In a large mixing bowl combine the cornmeal, flour, soda, salt and pepper. In a small bowl combine the milk, egg and oil and blend carefully. Pour the liquid into the dry mix and stir with a spoon. Add the drained jalapeños and stir once more to distribute evenly. Pour the batter into the mold and bake for 25 minutes. The cornbread is done when the top is colored.

Pâté Salt For Ducks and Geese

1 tablespoon freshly cracked black pepper
1 tablespoon freshly cracked white pepper
1 tablespoon ground nutmeg
1 tablespoon ground mace
1 tablespoon ground cloves

2 teaspoons mild paprika
2 teaspoons ground cayenne pepper
2 teaspoons ground marjoram
2 teaspoons thyme

Blend the spices carefully. Salt may be added to the foregoing to taste. This makes about 1 cup of pâté salt for ducks and geese, also known as *quatre épice*. Can be stored in an airtight jar for several months.

GIBLET GRAVY

1 cup goose giblets (gizzard, heart and neck bone), liver
  reserved
2 cups water
1 onion, chopped
½ teaspoon dried thyme
1 clove garlic, mashed

½ carrot, chopped
½ rib celery, sliced
Salt and pepper
2 tablespoons butter
2 teaspoons arrowroot

To make the giblet gravy, simmer the neck and giblets in the water, along with the onion, thyme, garlic, carrot, celery and salt and pepper to taste. After 2 hours, strain the stock and set it aside. Chop the heart and gizzards and add them to the stock. Sauté the liver in the butter, chop it and add to the gravy if desired. To thicken the gravy, mix the arrowroot with an equal portion of cold stock or water. Stir gently into the sauce off the heat, making sure there are no lumps. Return the pan to the stove and heat, stirring occasionally, until the gravy is of desired thickness.

APPLESAUCE QUEBEÇOISE

4 tart apples, peeled, cored and cut in ½-inch slices
1 tablespoon whole cloves
1 cup plus 2 tablespoons brown sugar, divided
¾ cup water
3 tablespoons lemon juice

1 tablespoon dark rum
1 lemon rind, grated
¼ teaspoon ground cloves
½ teaspoon ground cinnamon

Use enough apples to line and fill the bottom of a baking pan one layer only. Adorn each apple slice with a whole clove stuck near the middle. Boil 1 cup of the brown sugar and the water to make a syrup, about 3 to 5 minutes. Add lemon juice and pour over the apples.

In a preheated 350°F oven bake the apples for 45 minutes, or until tender. Sprinkle the rum over the apples, then the remaining brown sugar, the lemon rind, the ground cloves and the cinnamon. Place under the broiler for 10 minutes, or until all the sugar is caramelized.

NARY PROCEDURES ILLUSTRATEI

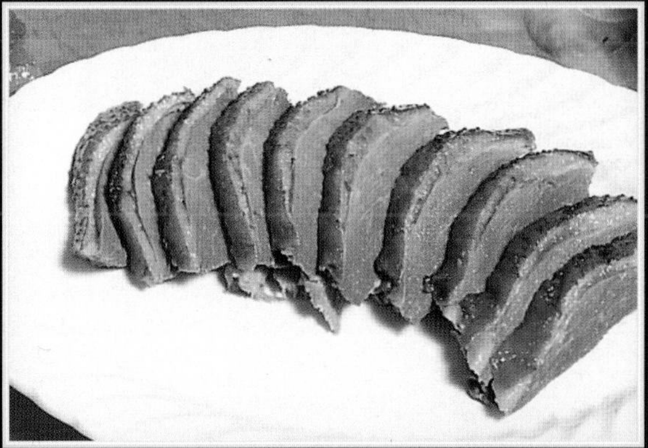

CARVING THE ROAST GOOSE OR DUCK

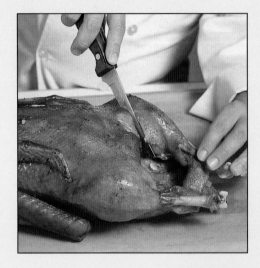

1.

When the bird has reached an internal breast meat temperature of 145°F the meat will be rare, but the legs will still be raw at the second joint. When the internal second joint temperature is 160°F the bird will be cooked throughout and should be taken from the oven and allowed to rest on a warm platter for 10 minutes before carving.

2.

With the bird breast up, using a narrow, pointed knife, cut off the legs at the hip joint. This is done by circling the skin at the base of the leg with the blade of the knife cutting down to the hip joint. The joint is opened with the tip of the knife, and the remaining skin separated. Place the legs on a separate platter, and return to the oven for further cooking if necessary.

3.

Remove the wings with a narrow, pointed knife by circling the skin at the base of the wing, and cutting down to the joint. Separate as with the leg.

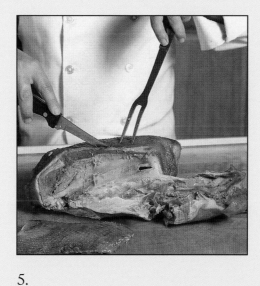

4.

Repeat the removal of each leg and wing on the opposite side of the bird in the same fashion.

5.

To remove the entire breast, begin on one side with a vertical cut as close to the breastbone as possible, cutting down and along the length of the breast, and then filleting out the entire breast in one piece. Repeat the process on the other side.

6.

Arrange the carved slices in a fan-shaped pattern, slightly overlapping one another, leaving space for the garnish and supporting recipe components.

BREASTING THE BIRD AND BRINGING THE BONE

  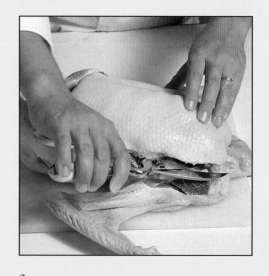

1.

With the bird fully picked and cleaned, use a sharp, pointed knife to cut the skin in a line running from just above one wing, down below the breast meat on one side, and following a straight line to the cavity. Repeat this cut on the other side.

2.

Using a pair of kitchen shears follow the two cuts previously made, clipping through the ribs and cartilaginous tissue along the sides of the breasts.

3.

Continue clipping, until you reach the collar bone. Then, using a sharp, pointed knife, separate the collar bone from the carcass at the outside points of the "Y" at the shoulder socket.

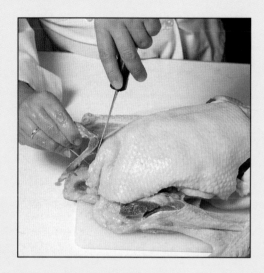  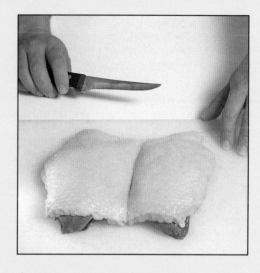

4.

Using the point of a sharp knife remove the wishbone from the breast.

5.

Lift the double breasts in one hand and separate the remaining skin and tissue connecting to the carcass with a knife.

6.

The pair of breasts with bone in may be braised as is, or separated by filleting each breast from the bone, and splitting the skin.

BONING THE DUCK FOR A BALLOTINE

1.

Skin the duck beginning with a midline cut down the backbone. Work around the wing and leg, dislocating the joint of each with the tip of a small knife. Stop when you reach the breastbone on one side, and repeat the process on the other side.

2.

Holding the carcass aloft, carefully slice through the cartilaginous material that connects the skin to the breastbone, allowing the skin and meat to fall free. Pare the meat from the legs and wings, discarding the bones.

3.

Arrange the duck skin side down. Fill the cavity between the two breasts with leg and wing meat scraped from the bone. Then layer the skin with cabbage and a few stalks of fennel.

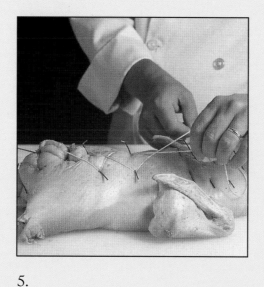

4.

Spoon the sausage mixture over the vegetables, and spread evenly.

5.

Form the roll (or ballotine) by bringing the sides of the original incision together from side to side to recreate the original form of the duck. Fold over and secure the flaps at the head and tail ends with small poultry skewers and even out the sides of the roll, lacing the ballotine carefully with cotton string.

6.

Cook on top of the stove in a large skillet with 1 cup of duck fat over moderately high heat, turning several times and basting with a spoon. When the ballotine has a crispy, rich brown color it is done. Allow to cool before removing skewers and string. Slice transversely into ½-inch slices.

BUILDING THE TERRINE MAISON

1.

After placing a decorative bay leaf shiny side down on the bottom of the empty terrine, line the interior of the terrine with pork fatback thinly sliced.

2.

Mix the ground forcemeat, egg and spices thoroughly with your hands, incorporating all the bits without reducing the particle size.

3.

Pack half of the forcemeat into the terrine carefully, compacting the mixture to avoid air spaces.

4.

Create a layer of the whole breast meat slices, leaving some space between the slices.

5.

Cover the forcemeat with more fatback, and then a layer of foil. Place the terrine in a bain marie, or larger oven dish that will hold 1 inch of boiling water, prior to introducing the terrine into a preheated 350°F oven for 2 hours.

6.

When the cooked terrine is removed from the oven allow it to cool slightly, and then carefully remove the foil. Place a new foil cover over the terrine, and then place a weight on the terrine and allow it to stand overnight. The weighting is important in producing a dense forcemeat that slices easily.

SUPPLIERS

American Institute of Wine & Food
1550 Bryant Street, Suite #700
San Francisco, California 94103-4832
(415) 255-3000

Grimaud Farms of California
1320-A South Aurora Street
Stockton, California 95206
(209) 466-3200

Bridge Kitchenware
214 52nd Street
New York, New York 10022
(212) 838-1901

Czimer's Game and Sea Foods, Inc.
13136 W 159th Street
Lockport, Illinois 60441-8767
(708) 301-0500

D'Artagnan, Inc.
280 Wilson Avenue
Newark, New Jersey 07105
(973) 344-0565

Fare Game Food Company
P.O. Box 18431
Rochester, New York 14618
(716) 473-4210

Manchester Quail Farms
P.O. Box 97
3525 Camden Highway
Dalzell, South Carolina 29040
(800) 845-0421

Matfer Kitchen and Bakery Equipment Co.
16249 Stagg Street
Van Nuys, California 91406
(818) 782-0792

"Butchers to the Stars"
Morris Lobel & Sons, Inc.
1096 Madison Avenue
New York, New York 10028
(800) 5-LOBELS • (212) 737-1372

POLARICA (game, poultry and berries)
105 Quint Street
San Francisco, California 94124
(800) GAME-USA

Williams-Sonoma Inc.
P.O. Box 7456
San Francisco, California 94120-7456
(800) 541-2233

INDEX